EAST WALNUT HILLS

EMILY SPENCER

EAST WALNUT HILLS

EMILY SPENCER

ZONE 3 PRESS
Clarksville, Tennessee

Library of Congress Cataloging-in-Publication Data

Names: Spencer, Emily, 1992- author.
Title: East Walnut Hills / Emily Spencer.
Identifiers: LCCN 2021024474 | ISBN 9781733150545 (paperback)
Subjects: LCGFT: Poetry.
Classification: LCC PS3619.P46433 E27 2021 | DDC 811/.6--dc23
LC record available at https://lccn.loc.gov/2021024474

ISBN: 9781733150545

Cover Art by **Adam Mysock** – "Attempt at Imperfect Optimism"
Book and Cover Design by **David Bieloh**

CONTENTS

NEIGHBOR 1

I. **THE VIEW**

PARK 5
SKY 6
TOWER 7
UPPER OVERLOOK 8
BLUEPRINT 9
WALK 10
WEATHER REPORT 11
AMPHITHEATER 14
OVERLOOK AT NIGHT 15
UNIVERSE 17
SEASON 18
SHOW 19

II. **THE SCHOOL**

NAME 23
DISCOVERY 24
STUDY 25
PHOENIX 26
SHAPE 27
STUDY ABROAD 28
BIBLIOTHECA 29
BLUE CLAY 30
THE KID DRESSED EXACTLY LIKE ME 31
DRAMA 32
PERMISSION 33

III. **THE AUTHORITY**

POWER 37
PLOUGH 38
CAPITAL 39
FOUNTAIN SQUARE 40
STATUE TO BE REMOVED 41
I'M NOT INTERESTED 42
PEDESTAL 43
BLACK LAURA 45

IV. **THE CREATION**

PERMANENT COLLECTION 49
SPECIAL EXHIBIT 50
CLAY 52
SANTA MARIA NOVELLA 53
FORM 54
COPIES 56

V. **THE PLAN**

EVACUATION 59
THESIS 60
GPS 61
SECOND PASSION 64
EXPANSION 65
OVER-THE-RHINE 66
MANIFEST 67

VI. **THE EXCHANGE**

BUTTERFLIES 71
MARKET 72
NEIGHBORHOOD STORE 73
STADIUM I 74
STADIUM II, DRAFT 75
COMMON SENSE 82
MIRROR LAKE 83

VII. **THE LIFE**

NO SAINT 89
CRUCIBLE STEEL 91
MARWIN LAKE 92
TRENDS 95

GASLIGHT DISTRICT 97

ACKNOWLEDGEMENTS 99
AFTERWORD 100
RESOURCES 101

Ubuntu
I am because we are.

"Bringing the gifts that my ancestors gave,
I am the dream and the hope of the slave. I rise."

—Maya Angelou

"You write in order to change the world...if you alter, even by a millimeter, the way people look at reality, then you can change it."

—James Baldwin

"It falls on all of us, regardless of our race or station...to work together to create a 'new normal' in which the legacy of bigotry and unequal treatment no longer infects our institutions or our hearts."

—Barack Obama

This book of poetry contains statistics from the Pew Research Center and *Psychology of Women Quarterly*. It references the U.S. Constitution.

NEIGHBOR

The Earth is cloud marbled, inscribed with sea.
Orion, big unbothered company.

An end to 1,000-foot descents, the black
blistering plastic bucket-swing—use cracked.

A place, round, for viewing all the sides.
Today, the temp's so high. It's ninety. *Writhe.*

The truth's a coyote spotted in Eden.
Our sky—slate gray—it swiftly conquers even,

"It's cold, a bit, in here," this maze tower.
A summit—nationless—eschews power.

Neighborhood: lines. The hills unfurled are East.
On Woodburn, glance at changed houses for lease.

At Walnut Hills, the geeks recite Shakespeare.
"He wants to bomb the hood," they overhear.

A statue throws a discus nowhere, quick,
to fall asleep, awake, and birth a ship.

Studio art: the river clay is form.
Abroad they sell Politely Black and squirm.

Ex Libris: Study Tables: rockets—strange.
In Walnut Hills, "The Dream" we sought: deranged.

THE VIEW

PARK

Truth is a coyote
spotted in Eden Park, slinks mythic
across the millennial playground—

its bright light reflective eyes,
its shadowy frame. It creeps
like misfit marginalizeds made to slink

through our Queen City crowned
by Great American's light-up tiara
pink and green and perfect

on a skyscraper built by a family
whose business is to be richer
than hundreds of families

who work and die within Cincinnati's
borders. Borders, according to a mural
in Over-the-Rhine, are here destroyed,

not by stone
but by love.

SKY

The sky—slate gray—it conquers even
seeing rusted objects for golden God
in East Walnut Hills. Mourning winds,

they whip the windows wet-beaded with glass
droplets as brick Victorians bloom against
the blur of rain not shot from Cupid's bow.
            bow: rape's apologizer

The wind whimpers, whistles, and woes,
O, woah, woah, wooo, oo,
as if a lonely graying troubadour

stuck like a fly in the screen. Aperture
between the flooded neighborhood and
underworld open, so the gusts—they gore

my bright black writing room in a high-rise whose
pipe breath requires repair from the hard labor
of rising above the dun mud-glutted Ohio,

a river unapologetically bodacious,
above the Northern Kentucky toy houses
and yellow arch of the bridge, Big Mac,

which sticks out, the rind of a yellow
watermelon—*on a sunny day, holy.*

TOWER

It is cold, a bit, in here—this maze tower.
Labyrinthine, the Brinkpoint condo: solitary
or nuptial space of housing, heartbeats, door

alongside door, a lift to floors, the steel
gate open to this neighborhood: streets of place
upon place all winding up and down the gray hills.

It is only a bitter cool in East Walnut Hills
as late December eggshell clouds are without
snow. The degrees are oddly autumnal, feverish

at fifty-four Fahrenheit. *The low tonight*
is thirty-eight, as the rains rain relentless
and the wind sweeps detritus off the cement bridge,

claiming Eden Park as ours. The bridge:
an aqueduct into and out of downtown.
The park: our tree-thick Midwestern paradise—

no West Coast inferno. For now,
we have no Santa Ana fears,
no tinderbox tendencies.

Romulus and Remus in bronze suckle
the teats of a she-wolf in Eden Park.

UPPER OVERLOOK

pinnacle—nationless
butterflies

a mythology of butterflies
a mythology of trees

BLUEPRINT

The neighborhood, lines.
The hills just hills. East
directive, near pure.

Blue laminated hill.
The old water tower looms,
red-bricked. Draw a gentrified

ancient neighborhood. Fill in
creation, erase slaughter,
highlight the resurrection

of black Christ on a Baptist
church in the remainder
miniature gray hood.

The Brinkpoint condo has *always
been there* gilded and the gray
Palms project too by Marathon

gas station. Pumping fuel
rich alongside poor, *can't
last.* A realtor, business man,

hair shellacked back, frowns at
a smiling prostitute, a business
woman in red fishnets, he calls,

whore. How to draw a hand
blue and wide-palmed
over everything without

power, windblown—
hands tied and sat on.

WALK

on Woodburn, there are changed houses
for punch, ale, but not the mass-evicted poor,
the most evicted: poor black folk, the ran away.
    You may not belong

here you may not belong here though
once: safe houses. I don't sit long at the bar
among salmon-shorted friends with pink

cheeks yelling about America,
wearing worn political caps—
you might drink yourself akin to—

and they may stare at brown skin
until it's political. They may pretend
this street wasn't Jewish or black,

native or nobody's. Money buys
Woodburn bars and the salmon-
shorted men claim it's boom and bust,

the ropes. This time, they tell truth.
They sigh. Take a walk on Woodburn
with a smiley face full of strangled

teeth among ale-drunk disillusioned
anarchists with empty eyeglasses,
ironic rap, and frail tolerance for black.

You can belong here in the tourist store or you can
not belong here in a concrete square among school kids
walked out, peacefully protesting brute police.

A woman can move wherever the hell
she wants, says a hipster barista, Jen.
I wish I could break this century's cruel lease

with kindness. Neighbor, I don't belong to
a neighborhood. Can somebody let me in?

WEATHER REPORT

It will
feel

high
today:

92,
it will feel 100,

it will feel
misery: humidity.

The flood and the fog.

Dark cream over green-populated
Queen City parks. Erased
towers. There are no monarchs

of this nation. There is
a chance of flood. Of
dictators. Beware high
incoming water, sudden force.

The flood and the fog.

Of chance:
chance of
chance of lime
ripening to rot
chances
the changed
chance listing
on the century
changing votes
changelings
chant chance of
rain of rust of

the flood and the fog.

The doors to Saint Francis cathedral
are always locked. Architecture of loss.
Church: pretty on a hill: a bell ringing.
Limestone Gothic. Teal copper steeple. 100
feet tall, cross piercing smog. Chance of:

the flood and the fog

and Satan sealing shut 30-foot doors
(engraved Judgement) as a priest
watches a child outside, drowning.

The flood and the fog.

There is a chance some believers
think *some people look like*
they have no religion—get locked out.
Their church is nature.

The flood and the fog.

It feels: hell. It feels: heaven
in here: a there: in this wet East
Walnut Hills, humid, as if hugged
tight by a persistent lord: mother: snake.

The flood and fog.

Some people deliver
news of weather
as if the word of God,
It is the word of God
spoken in every language,
God breathed, wind.

The flood and the fog.

The wind under our feet:
our weather report. We listen
every day and make the sign
of peace past locked doors.

The flood and the fog.

Did you know it is a downpour?
Did you know the poor fall poorly—
richly—and the rich fall rarely poor?
we ask desperately as if reading
scripture alone as the rain pours
salvation upon
solution upon
sin snaking
obviously down
office windows,

shelter
walls

AMPHITHEATER

Αμφιθέατρο

a place, round, to view
from all sides. Descend—

here: new mother, new child
accidentally perform love,
sitting on a stage eating bread.

Is love listening
as a child dressed exactly
like you delights? *Look!*

See, a bird—flying!
Is to love to watch
a tiny finger point east,

track a bird over Mirror
Lake and above to gray
heights? *Grandma.*

Departed, I have been spent
alone in this body. I have spent
so much to be loved like this.

The child, bread-faced,
kisses the mother's hair
as if a monarch's crown.

Is loving to hold your own hand
as if the child's? I have not spent
much to love myself like this.

Red-leashed, a dog walks
itself on stage, circles,
more wolf than friend.

OVERLOOK AT NIGHT

Green plastic bucket-swings—
sun spotted, cracked,
near-fragrant under cider lamplight—

a wolf toy head-
first in the mulch,
by and by and by

motorcycles against the dark—
red-eyed, flanks star-glazed—country
roaring from our lone station.

Until an officer barricades our Upper
Overlook, pushes a swing, smokes
overlooking the black

great river, Ohio, *ohi:yo',*
Seneca for great river—body
of water: reflective, silent soul.

soil
Seoul
soil

Soil is
pronounced soul
in these parts.

He contemplates the sprint
downhill, the swim too far out.

Is what it feels like to be dead
what it feels like to be black?

The officer takes off his vest,
stomps out a cigarette in litter,
practices the butterfly, away and farther.

Maybe there will be quiet
Maybe judgement will come

Inside the boney barracks of
my Eden, there is no force

only nature and nobody
moves except by eastern tiger,

spicebush, swallowtail, painted
lady, or

in green bucket-swings—perpetual
summer, perpetual day and night.

UNIVERSE

Earth, cloud-marbled,
blue green in a black

womb forever, rotates
daily faster than sound

as the sun summits
in heavens to wake

us, in East Walnut Hills, gold
rays remind us to ask why

we seek out gold
from the Earth's bowels

—to be like waking.
Why we run about in night

—to be like Earth
moving in the dark. *Why,*

as the sun glitters on wet
city roads? Why, when night

swaddles us rolling
into bed and the grave?

Likeness—to be like that which is.
Gold rings. Black shadows dancing.

What lasts longer than day or night
is heaven knows. Beyond now,

my grandma's limitless
kind hands time-traveled.

Goodness knows goodness
justifies reality—unless

we are wolves in playgrounds
as energy and matter persist.

Unless we don't ask why the darkest lady
is settled by mankind's myths by its lust

not love as the Earth grows, lives,
and dies within her—or he or they.

How many great nights
have I given away?

It is hard to breathe
with everyone's hands at their throat.

SEASON

& the birds
remained still engraved
long late fall heat

SHOW

Milky Way, indifferent sparkly
company—red
fireworks over the Ohio, heart-shaped

in smoky, gray shared-heavens—North, South.
Black veins,
trees' silhouettes against illuminated hilltop,

see the yellow clay exposed. See the slid
land.
How we forget the Earth gives   way.

THE SCHOOL

NAME

At Walnut Hills High School, a figure—marble,
muscular—throws a discus nowhere down
a checker-floored hall or somewhere

at bay forever or just for now
and the pupils read *Apology*
are given Latin names then Spanish then French.

When a seventh grader wants to change her name
from Momitul to Ma'Rhea or Mary, her peers—
they cringe and can't recite the root of cringe.

They tell her that her name before renaming
was beautiful and strange. A student who was
then *wasn't* the future

valedictorian tells her humans
are beautiful and strange, eats a whole
free school lunch in English class, is sent to

the office for insubordinate feasting
then cites a private illness rage-
and-hunger, blames the English teacher

for teaching: how to wonder what happens
to a self among selves in East Walnut Hills.

Momitul reclaims renaming and shames
her peers for their renaming-shaming,
changes her name to Decision Mine

then decides Momitul is just fine after re-
breaking a model of the known universe.

Her peers recite apologies until
they believe in them, until
asked for original lamentation.

DISCOVERY

there was a ship in my bathtub
then rabbit bones in the sink
underneath the sink a planet
by the baseboards telephone
booths and in my bed dolls

everywhere I looked
I could not remember why
I was looking or what for
so I said *simply amazing*
and fell asleep on the couch

upon waking I saw a kid
dressed exactly like me

STUDY

At Walnut Hills High, geeks recite Shakespeare.
In the forum, they build bridges to hold
free weights. Independently, full of self-

critical empathy and numbers, after
school before junior varsity sports and stag
school dances, drugs and bullying,

deflowering-lies, they study how to
pronounce Momitul obsessively with self-
flagellation because they study to make

sense of loneliness and pain. Study
The Times and justice, war, science, they study
blocking out death and loss. They study

everything desperately even debating
everything, debating the study of Latin
at Walnut Hills—*in nomine Patris*

et Filii et Spiritus Sancti. They go to
a mock trial juried by uninterested peers
and claim, defense and prosecutor, Latin

is beautiful and strange in East Walnut Hills
or maybe nothing is beautiful and strange
in the known universe—everything is ugly

and cannot solve its own loneliness. Though
Jamaal, studying Zen, claims loneliness
resides in the self. He checks for it daily.

Finds nothing but senses
he's getting close.

PHOENIX

They want to bomb Avondale?
A phoenix is a mythological creature.

Phoenix isn't in the hills—it hugs.
Robotics wins against Walnut. Fake-

gold trophies line hallways like liberation.
T'Chyna writes *HOW DO U LIBERATE*

SOMETHING THAT'S BURNIN ALIVE?
Her teacher writes, *No yelling. Good question.*

A phoenix liberates itself with extreme
strength. Sometimes the scholars feel
they are freezing and drowning.

What do you know about Avondale?
It is 90% black and over 40% poor.

What do you know about Phoenix?
Truth is we ain't a mythological creature.

The scholars will build truth robots
after they pass the state test, after
they manage the world's trauma.

The teachers feel modern saints
and Avondale: society's martyr,
mule—forgotten, brilliant prophetic kin.

SHAPE

In studio art, *blue clay is form,*
a teacher says, *and solid wet woe*
touched to joy.

Something about true love
singing in the spun hold, *to collect not*
capture: East Walnut Hills, a red rose.

Joan, class clown, breaks a blue vase full of
fake flowers. *This is radical love,* she says.
The custodian asks, *What about real roses?*

Outside, Ohio River clay is blued
under fingernails. You imagine
a world with blue as blanket

adjective. Blue hills, blue unpolluted
river. Blue sky, the symbol for awe.

STUDY ABROAD

They sell Civilization, sell Art,
growl at us

as if a pack of hungry wolves
afraid of eating themselves.

BIBLIOTHECA

Every cherry
table a spaceship,

This is the future: this
is the future. The future

is bright—slaughterhouse
of blue youth ignorance,

row upon row of racks
emptied to a cloud.

Of echoes, even the sound
of librarians' clogs

clacking, their, *Quiet.*
Be quiet, please, might

quiet. Will we be able to
turn off our ears

to silence the hate?
To turn off our minds

to violence? *Silence!*
Teacher? *Yes.* Would you die

for us? *What?* Human shield.
Yes, the teacher says, points

to extreme weather plans,
It's in the protocol. Now,

look up and look up
how to surrender to love.

Download survival, sleep
on dove-feathered marble,
rose-bloodied floor.

BLUE CLAY

In East Walnut Hills, life is beautiful
and strange. We mine our experiences
and beget empathetic blue clay

to make our precious bowls
in the hot kiln, a churn core,
of the Rookwood Pottery in Mount Adams.

Descending the green hills are teenagers, green
street vendors offering knock-offs
of these clay artifacts of contemporary blues.

Knock-offs made in the kilns of Walnut Hills
High School by the lone woke poor black
kid or white or gray in the AP Art class.

They are testing how much
they can take to the fire
and retrieve uncracked.

They are busy Lauras.
They are busy making Lauras,
making Letishas, making Ka'Nishas

making Kyles and Gagans and
Dragons. Busy mayors of the fiery soul
forcing the body out of bed at 6 am,

come to Walnut Hills bookbags slung
over one shoulder in a nation deemed
the place of dreams in the dreamland

to make these beautiful bowls
used to catch our millennial tears in style.

THE KID DRESSED EXACTLY LIKE ME

Boston, MA

is asking for money.
I don't know how to say, *No,*

I don't have it. I go on dates
to sleep out of the cold. I fear night,

all day, and take the kid on superheated
subways full of light to Free Sunday

but the kid is clingy and won't play
even sandcastles or water.

DRAMA

21st century—ignorant humans in
the brightest of ages—puppets, stage.
Everywhere I go I study the same play.

PERMISSION

Cambridge, MA

The cover of *TIME*
is ENOUGH.

DR. DIVINITY: *Kids are like arrows*
we launch into our world for good

or evil. Go forth, all the kids
I'll never birth. All the men
I'll never marry. Women I tried

to befriend. Aloft, peace replaces arms.
If I die, bury my soul in marked clouds,
enough for God to find me.

THE AUTHORITY

POWER

In Cincy, Mayor Black's a former senator
who can't translate *sursum ad summum* and
who people know of but who isn't known

by many people. So it is, we don't ponder if,
at Walnut Hills, the mayor was a geek or
uninterested juror, as long as we know

the mayor is known enough to trust.
The mayor, godlike, and developers, gods,
fidget with our neighborhood and raw resources.

Our mayor's everywhere: multiplicity
of flora and fauna spun out of Krohn
Conservatory's glass dome in Eden Park.

He is undercover in Presidents' Grove,
underneath past presidents' trees. Is a mayor
a Washington if shaded by George Washington oak?

Our mayor is two hundred and eighty-three,
a dying Brinkpoint condo president says, eighty
and bald from chemo. *Elm,* his wife declares

as she puts stone cold hands over the dead
man's, her dead partner's, unblinking eyes.

PLOUGH

We all pull the steel plough.

CAPITAL

The mayor's father lived on Millionaire's Row,
up from the hood, on Northern Kentucky's banks,
up from the South, up from enslaved. For Ohio's

The Banks, the mayor cuts red ribbon
to open: skyscrapers, in glass glazed
blue, and adds or subtracts from the budget.

The budget is second to God here
—then crime and punishment.

FOUNTAIN SQUARE

Glass woman: fountain,
tossing water into the air,

still tosses water in the air
as the armed gunman is shot

dead by police. People are
in the streets looking for God.

STATUE TO BE REMOVED

At Sawyer Point, in Bicentennial
Square, hundreds of feet below the gray
hills, Cincinnatus stands patina bronze,

in contrapposto forever, on a pink
granite base. War survived. Touches
a wood-grained plough. Offers

his dictator's fasces, axe and rod,
to pigeons and people shhffting by.
They slap his smooth limbs with

their feathers and leather huddled into
their bird-breasts against the wind
by the banks as the Ohio River rises

to seep into Northern and Southern
pores. Cut-outs, black silhouettes
of pigeons and people and dictators

are blown up the walls into the gaslit
golden streets of East Walnut Hills.

I'M NOT INTERESTED

Gold

Circles

Third phalanges

Bernini's Baroque

Canopy in St. Peter's

Gold

Circles

The aftermath of sun

On the eye

Lid shut

To an exposed window

Her blue eye always opens

Wide wider across his shoulder

Across the world wider

I could look at you both *forever*

At you all in the black pupils

Encircled

Glinting

Hallelujah and never fall in love

Or consume

Your Eucharist

Pietà in the Vatican

With conviction cradles

Christ

PEDESTAL

Eve stands before Eden
Park fourteen feet tall

on a four-foot base,
points forever down

at a limestone snake. Beware
there are snakes in the grass.

In the grass, there are snakes. This
is the statue that bleeds at night.

Bare white marble forever
against a huge glass window.

Face man-carved
with shame and fear.

This is the statue that leans
as if to lean out of herself.

This is our mythic beauty.
Unconsenting. Uncontested.

This is the statue that screams
at night, against composure.

In the grass, in Kentucky,
there are snakes. In the grass,

everywhere, snakes. In Boston,
on sidewalks. Without a platform,

without sculpture's pause,
in perpetual escape,
a black woman is bitten and dies.

In death, rigor mortis
turns her into stone.

Her matriarch, a black grandma, towers
atop an AstroTurf porch in low pumps

on unaired news in a shapeless
church dress, bombarded by cameras,

her hair neatly set in metal curlers,
as if to say, *I know you eternally*

are waiting to capture my collapse.
A big black church hat obscures

her face. Speaking to a cameraman
crouched below in her rose bed,

she points down at the twice-
mowed diamond grass, *Honey,*

there are snakes
in the grass. Beware!

BLACK LAURA

The mayor is bronze, the North Star, Christ.
The Mayor Black exists, like the white
unicorn in the Cincinnati Art Museum

set on a peak overlooking East Walnut
Hills, high as a ziggurat, telling us what
is beautiful. The white unicorn appears

in a Raphael painting of probably Laura—
this time, not Petrarch's Laura but
a Laura loved and objectified

as reliquary and relic, like not any
Laura immortalized in pigment and lighting,
like a Laura we'd all love to be

as a premise—but not forever
on a wall nailed up and guarded
by security as couples make out

shamelessly before us, becoming what
we most desired: imperfect and full
of quenchable want. Not many women get

to be guarded by men who ask for nothing
in return but Laura is a masterpiece
and she doesn't mention the price

is captivity. Mayor Black is a busy
Laura, probably, or else the Channel 5
news would say, *The mayor is dead.*

In East Walnut Hills, we don't wonder
what happens if the black Lauras run out.

THE CREATION

PERMANENT COLLECTION

Over East Walnut Hills, a semi-secular
acropolis, Mount Adams, rises out of
Eden Park with theaters, bars, and churches.

Just before the sign *Welcome*
to Mount Adams on the liminal peak,
the crown of East Walnut Hills, sits

an old stone building—the Cincinnati
Art Museum. Inside, a Sabine woman,
twenty-three inches tall, in bronze,

is raped over and over
by Rome's founders.

SPECIAL EXHIBIT

No touching.
The guard guards
her and him—him
behind her before
bodies poised for war:
arms drawn back,
kneeling, crouching
expressionless
excavated soldiers.
Terracotta figures of
eight thousand figures,
eternity embodied—
inanimate grave
shells, no shoreline.
No touching,
she says to him—
him behind her,
watching noon sunlight
illuminate her onyx iris
looking at bronze
figurines black-
colored, shining
and leaping lithely
as if white
plaster molds.
Don't touch
this art,
her to him.
Him to her,
We live in an awesome
time, and her
to him, *A terrible*
time, and him to her, *No,*
we have everything now.
Him behind her—before
white marble serpent
and Eve in an alcove
as he suppresses his twang,
as he suppresses his Kentucky
twang and she mispronounces
cuneiform in the Near East
gallery. Her before him—
and before art
museum farewell
when they had sex deep

in Kentucky, *Touch me.*
Trust me.
She mistook a Greek
nose for blackness
and sex
for love.
Beyond back then, him
behind her—before statue
of compassion and wisdom,
multi-armed god,
the guard says, *No*
touching! No touching.
You are worlds
apart.

CLAY

In East Walnut Hills, time is our natural
disaster yet a raw resource like clay,
inquiry, and flesh. From creeks pouring

into the cold Ohio River riddled
with ghosted fugitive slave bones—upstream,
bordered with *Thamnopora* fossil beds taking

in heroin needles when water levels rise, we make
pottery; we made pottery. On mugs, you won't
find Classical rapes—you won't find rapes.

You find progress in relief informed by
perhaps the beauty and terror
of history as information showers

us from Ohio to Neolithic to Prehistoric, from
the 2001 riots to Tubman, from Civil War to Ur.

SANTA MARIA NOVELLA

Florence, Italy

Outside the Santa Maria Novella basilica, I draw belief
in God for hours on a bench and local and foreign
visitors watch me watching faith. We all stare down

the church. Revisit and retrace an object
as if it can save the millennium, as if it can save me.
I am drawing to you, Love, in straight black lines

as a spectator's wrinkles deepen. Who is on the watch
for angels and Satan as millennials take self-portraits
filtered to Beautiful for hours in front of the church?

As if to Follow as if to Like as if to Share as if to Friend
as if to Capture as if to Block as if to Leak. Is this social
media faith's purgatory? *Please believe in my selves.*

Inside my real body, frescoes. Frescoes and sketches of
now dead little i's and little u's then purportedly loving.
Love™– a façade as flat as the green and white lines

mapping the face of the Santa Maria Novella.
All one hundred people in this square freeze
to view order for seconds and minutes and hours

and the lovers kiss and hold it as if Love's relics
as I wonder who will be discarded upon homecoming as
if trash blown up the dew-slicked streets of East Walnut Hills.

u and i kissed and held it for years
in America to peel off the black and white
color scheme on Satan's dividing palette yet

my image you displayed for no one. Unaffirmed,
unshared, you ghosted me. Our love — my grave.

Behind the basilica, the sinking sun births shadow-
twins, keeps loneliness company. Couples go silently
away. Nights, I pretend to be loved™—paint God.

Where the tour

Where the auction

FORM

At Walnut Hills High, Jamaal works
at lunch in The Commons under cover
underneath blue tarps tented to Alps.

Honors Italy trip: he saw copies,
plaster, of Roman busts and David
fourteen feet tall, huge-headed

a copied man towering above Palazzo Vecchio,
skin grayed by shit. Original David stands
white in the Galleria dell' Accademia,

the inanimate man's home. *Hey Jerome,*
what are you afraid of? the preps ask and
ask to copy tests for History, peer over blue,

claim they've seen the heart of darkness,
claim they can't see anything at all. Gravity
pulling them in and in on themselves,

folded. In folders, the Congo Basin test.
They sneak in Jamaal's tote
for answers as he cinches tarp.

The preps harp on Jamaal's paranoia
say he's lost his marbles, his cat's
eyes—a regular da Vinci, a Maya Angelou.

They say, what we have in common is
in part, The Commons, why has Jamaal gone
under the commons—didn't he study Rome?

They claim he's writing in code.
His letters shaped like fish, ankhs,
a crucifix, quasi-hieroglyphic,

they claim he's making a black hole,
a prism for innocents, *mass incarcerateds,*
painting the Last Judgment black

unlike what he saw while slurred *Negro*
by guards in the Sistine Chapel, *Negro,*
silencio, silence, and *Negro, silence,*

as Jerome was silent, in awe of the awful weather
report on his phone. In Ten Years: Flooded. Behind, a
white peer, Maverick, ventriloquizes in ~~Black~~LoudVoice.

They keep calling Jamaal, Jerome.
They keep calling Jerome, Jamaal.
Meanwhile, Jamaal skips school at school.

Momitul throws Jamaal's beloved halal hotdogs
over the blue tarp and claims he's not Jerome,
invents he's eating his skin and bones.

Steel tables slide down The Commons
under the blue, disappear. The Seniors
are indicted for school pranks, fear. *Thank*

God, Jamaal sighs, *high on the hill:*
everywhere, everyone a sign spirals.

COPIES

We find nothing, not even Jamaal's bones
to bury in our cemetery's, Spring Grove's, dug
grave. Tamika says, *Strange, lack is beautiful,*
            lack of death,

sits in front of the nothing left as if
in another dimension, an in-school
self-suspension. She's alive but stone.

A prep voted *Most Artistic* sets up green tarps
on The Commons paints his white face black
speaks on lack. He will later perform in Columbus,

Harlem, Rome as Jerome the Alone, a millionaire
by twenty, in *The Times.* For now, Tamika turns
her back and is voted *Most Beautiful and Strange.*

She chants about a worm hole. The preps
reach out but do not touch her huge hair.

THE
PLAN

EVACUATION

Tamika, in World Religion, is starting
a religion the teacher says is a cult—*North*
Star. The mayor defunds study abroad

and The Bank's Freedom Center. Claims
black kids have Rome Reaction, won't
listen, sit under the sun until they glisten,

have a socialization syndrome
on The Commons: sitting for hours
together as if Mt. Vesuvius, rock.

Mt. Vesuvius is due to erupt. It is not a question
of if, the tour guide said, *but when the African*
Plate subducted beneath the Eurasian boils

to burst. Tamika says, *no, what cracks*
in East Walnut Hills is a rebirth
for people—the deep womb,

black hole. To be massively
pulled together by love
and in The End there is moonlight

and in the end there is no bang
boom—just a rose to new now.

THESIS

The millennium is writing: *I don't know. I know neither now nor how, here nor why.*

GPS

without it
I would be lost anywhere.

Naturally, we are all lost, or,
naturally, we are all founders.

Therefore, buy clouds.
Methinks my phone spies on me.
Are we soon nobodies—

sold? On the stock exchange:
idea companies, others' great life
stories. To be creative, I buried
my phone in rice.

Then I built an ark, a moon,
another Earth, a baby self.

The baby self, I cradled.
It felt like a true masterpiece.

Soon there will be nowhere left
to go so we will buy escape-
scented candles and leave dying

in the cart for $10,000's, unaware
execution is illegal and midazolam,
Asleep Underwater, is out of stock.

We'll go on artisan walks.
We'll stuff ourselves with stuff.
We'll download others' identities,

we'll hoard antique shopping carts
and update our souls. Refresh
soul. Soul refreshing. Spun

circle. After all, there is ebb
and flow and museums and
revivals and revivals and museums
and burnt museums and burnt revivals.

An old-fashioned diva sells perfume in plaid
pants from the seventies every seventeen
years, *Style always comes back in style.*

There is a genocide museum.

There is a Rwandan genocide museum.
There is a Holocaust museum.
There is a Freedom Center.

One day, a lady dumps her severed hand,
2cm cellPhone rooted inside,

into Mirror Lake. She lives. We forget
her name and carry on #living the same.

Soon there will be voices in our head
and we must decide if it is God.

Everyone will be anyone even if only
in virtual reality. Power Simulation.

Everyone will be insufficiently liked
enough to like them so we'll all wait
breathless at bars, searching.

Until then, I am running in Eden Park
on break from technology and hair,
full-embodied—strapped to my jaw,
a smile, chipped and see-through

wailing, *Yippee!* See, you play
How-To-Be-Happy

and, suddenly, you are happy
or at least free until a man records it.

If we are recording, we are forgetting.
If we are hacking, we are spying.
In being online, we are off duty.

In being outside, we are on call,
the best ad at the Super Bowl,
selling you Natural Truth Tour.

Does it matter, truth? Naturally,
we will become and unbecome.
We will do and not do. Yet, the soul.

My yellow teeth are unlike reality TV
I watch to escape my reality or to live

or substitute for real bad company,
or to die of anxiety, to

be spent—to forget little i
is always happy to see me,

found dressed exactly
like me, with a map,
ever ready to take a nap.

SECOND PASSION

Firmly,
I believe
that if I were to lose
poetry
as a passion
if I had to choose
a second passion
it would be praying Madonna,
one of those women who
just sit there
in a dark church
in noon light
so alone
always beside themselves
like everyone in Cincinnati
is hilly and welcoming
like everyone in New York City
is intense and invaluable
praying and praying and praying
slowly emphatically quietly
staring into space,
lighting a candle,
kissing a symbol,
breathing.

EXPANSION

Eden Park returns you
return to yourself,
green alive
one-bodied.

In the hot-blooded
beating heart, the unquiet
unrequited soul, new Eden
grows—fathomless garden:

rose upon rose
upon row upon row of black
holes rimmed pink, whiff
of the perfume of witness:

the Here We Are No Place,
Entangled at Last. Forever.

Eden Park used to have
your heart. Now nature
expands within your breast.
There is no holy place name

for this
wild
park
thick with loss,

where in the shadow-canopy
of memory and folds of flesh
a coyote cries out *God, where am I?*
Who did I trample? Where are you

in the green god of nature's embrace
or *thy* laurels without a born witness?
This witness: Love. You had a love
and moved away to return to Eden

alone. In the something-bigger-than-Eden
of your brain, the trees sway with breath.

OVER-THE-RHINE

: time
on time
on time.

Ride the streetcar down to drink
in restored replacement places
drag a growler back up the hills.

Wrap up a universe in silk.
Come Monday, *I'll dig graves.*
You can bury me in Spring Grove.

Black dirt pitched
across the brow.

MANIFEST

Gallery houses *To Repeat,*
again and again idle hands
in "Idle Hands" in chiaroscuro.

If history repeats itself Adam
Mysock, I'll continue to live dead
feet-sunk in renovated Woodburn

staring at emerging artists
who never emerge out of
shallow silver plaques,

stay just behind too-late
names I know I'll forget yet snap
photographs to repeat hopeful

motion: a bright together, I
and the object. I and it, animate,
inanimate. *To Repeat,* in acrylic,

features blue, bluer, bluest
squares titled "An Attempt
at Imperfect Optimism."

I'm just another blue black
optimist walking white palm
in my other palm. As if arm

in arm with the invisible you
left outside of East Walnut Hills,
heart full of water. *To Repeat's*

painter is a local artist in residence.
I feel like an escape artist drowning.

THE EXCHANGE

BUTTERFLIES

for MarShawn McCarrell[1]

During the spring marathon, jogging by Krohn,
the street is pink, full of human
flying pigs. Petunias. If you run fast

enough from Walnut Hills START-lines you fly
out in commercial jets to coastal universities,
poverty tours, the Olympics in Brazil. If you

work hard or hardly enough you forget
you will die. Death pushes an empty silver
shopping cart weekdays, empty golden

stroller weekends, through the May *Butterfly!*
exhibit at Krohn Conservatory in Eden Park.
The monarchs are native and captive,

the beauty is native and captive,
Cincinnati is native and captive,
the world is native and captive—

they are, they aren't, the subjects continue
being trapped or protected, globally local.
Usually, Death passes by with, *Excuse me.*

Other times, Death taps your shoulder
while you gaze at giant prehistoric ferns,
looking for yourself in nature. *Very sorry,*

Death says retreating behind a fountain,
Krohn's mosaic tile fountain, in a city
with an outbreak of mosaic tile fountains,

which you feel like breaking your head
against, pixelated, as you get digital 24/7
news of a friend shooting himself dead

in front of the Statehouse. *Is it supernatural*
you scream—you don't scream, *to get away?*

1 MarShawn McCarrell, an Ohio activist and poet, founded Pursuing our Dreams and Feed the Streets. He attended the NAACP Image Awards and was honored for his activism, including involvement in the Black Lives Matter movement.

MARKET

Findlay Market in Over-the-Rhine:
over-the-counter
cold dead swine, brined.

In East Walnut Hills, deserted,
an American grocery elucidates
bare bone. Men solicit still.

WHAT FEEDS
THE HUMAN SPIRIT?
—graffiti over a billboard.

In the Amazon, Mount
Airy forest, trees fall
for everything desired,

please recycle this box.
Everyone hungers, at-home shops.
Soon, nobody leaves their cells.

Will there still be soup
kitchens in The Cloud?

Heaps of bakery bread expired
snuck past the poor to the dump
until the baker redirects the truck

and the human spirit. Holy
ghost, holy wasted dough—

to hunger: waste,
to starve: feast,
import flesh into flesh.

As the migrant laborer's heart over-
worked, underpaid stops, tomatoes
rot in crates for fast food troughs.

As the pigs scream in cages,
pesticides rain down on crops.

NEIGHBORHOOD STORE

To sell your neighborhood or to sell neighborhood
to vaguely unhappy remnants of a Lost Middle
Middle Class? I'd reluctantly sell Neighborhood
Store—selling neighborhood.
The store sells mustard-colored clocks or sells *whatever.*
Whatever you want I will sell.
I will sell you you
but I won't sell people.
I will sell you me
but I won't sell myself.
There are no souls available at this time.
I will write your brand
in heat across the horizon—
dirt red, risen with profit,
not prophet, profit.
Profit me whatever you want.
Email me or archaically mail
cards in a gold envelope titled "Whatever."
Inside the envelope, rainbow confetti seeps
sparkling-out as if to say *Hello, hello.*
When I go out of business
(because our business hung itself),
remember me like this: surprised, delighted.
Hello, how are you belonging here today?
Very well.
Thank you for shopping!

STADIUM I

The stadium is a ruin
the exchange students believe
stands far more complete
than the Colosseum—

under construction forever, rust
viewable downhill, an open wound
the wind whistles through as if the soul.

We are designing safer helmets.

The Colosseum is a ruin
the American pupils believe
stands far more complete
than the Grand Canyon.

STADIUM II, DRAFT

The Colosseum is a ruin
American pupils believe
stands far more complete
than the Grand Canyon.

We are designing
safer helmets.

The men are killing
themselves downtown. In
the stadium, you can view
them head to head to head.

In a few decades, they'll be poor
or senseless or dead. Heads full
of monsters—ghosts. Owned
played players playing victory.

Dear Most Valuable Players, I am not your fun
time. I am not a FunGirl.[2] *You are not having*
fun in my body[3] *for a Follow,*[4] *Friend, or wine.*

Brown player, afro-haloed, kneels
during the national anthem. Kneels.
He does not wage world war three

even as—knighted black—America
has not set him free, gladiator. America
is entertained by Black Knight aglow

as he kneels to her level. He:
Madonna. She: child, singing.

/The Empress of Soul, Gladys
Knight Sings at Halftime,
the National Anthem/where the knelt

---

2 "**We demonstrated that Black women are implicitly associated with both animals and objects to a greater degree than White women,**" *Psychology of Women Quarterly (Revisiting the Jezebel Stereotype: The Impact of Target Race on Sexual Objectification* by Anderson, Holland, Heldreth, and Johnson, 2018) [bold added]

3 *Psychology of Women Quarterly,* study noted, "**Recent research suggests that Black women are hypersexualized to a greater degree in the media than are White women.** For instance, Turner (2011) **analyzed the content of 120 music videos,** finding that Black women characters (both central and background characters) were significantly more likely to appear in provocative clothing than any other character type, including White women. Other content analyses have revealed **that Black women are typically depicted as hypersexual in rap music videos,** with an overemphasis on their sexualized physical appearance (e.g., Stephens & Phillips, 2003)." (Anderson, Holland, Heldreth, and Johnson, 2018) [bold added]

4 "**We sought to explore this across two distinct measures of objectification: the objectifying gaze and implicit associations with objects and animals.**" *Psychology of Women Quarterly* [bold added]

knight? *Where the dead innocent?*
Where the black folk[5] *enslaved*
in the prisons?[6]

Blackbird
—immortalized near flight,
thinking martyr

of Socrates
of Tubman

of aporia: red
blood clots black

black bodies bleed
to death unburied
on live screens

as we fear the police.[7]
Nobody will hire
the black player unsmiling, loving

humanity as if the evergreen Statue
of Liberty one hundred and fifty-one feet tall
backlit by New York City's glittery lights,
gone dark[8] against fog on Women's Day—

unsmiling face chiseled with justice,
this Libertas, Declaration—torch.

---

5 "In 2016, blacks represented 12% of the U.S. adult population but 33% of the sentenced prison population," John Gramlich, FactTank, Pew Research Center.

6 Constitution of the United States of America, Amendment XIII. Section 1, "Neither slavery nor involuntary servitude, except as a punishment for crime whereof the party shall have been duly convicted, shall exist within the United States, or any place subject to their jurisdiction."

7 *Vox:* "An analysis of the available FBI data by Dara Lind for Vox found that US police kill black people at disproportionate rates: **Black people accounted for 31 percent of police killing victims in 2012, even though they made up just 13 percent of the US population.**" *(There are huge racial disparities in how US police use force* by Germaine Lopez for *Vox,* 2018) [bold added]

8 Pew Research Center, "Two-thirds of police officers (67%) say the **highly publicized deaths of blacks** during encounters with the police are isolated incidents, while **31% describe them as signs of a broader problem.** Moreover, the survey finds that majorities of officers in virtually every major demographic group share this view, with one striking exception. **A majority of black officers (57%) say these deaths are evidence of a broader problem between police and blacks,** a view held by only about a quarter of all white (27%) and Hispanic (26%) officers. **Black female officers in particular** are more likely to say these incidents signal a more far-reaching concern. Among sworn officers, **63% of black women say this,** compared with 54% of black men." [bold added]

We do not have to be beautiful.
We just have to be Behemoths.[9]

As if in 1968, black-gloved Black Fastest
Men on Earth raise fists as if torches
for humanity during the national anthem,
their fellow white Olympian #2 badged too
in solidarity. *Survival is the greatest victory.*

Black American superstars neon backlit
by souls sing masterful songs full time
in North American stadiums under bright
lights in their own clouds advertising their
own dreams, half-owning their own music

their own immortal declarations of being
at war versus their fleeting lucrative stereotypes.[10]
They dance as if to resurrect the beheaded
players buried below snowy false turf.

We are refusing to play the game.

We are refusing to entertain you.[11]

In an ad, Serena Williams black in white
in her own green court, hits oppression[12]
with immense power over the heads of

---

9 Behemoths: The Bible, Job 40:15-24

10 *Psychology of Women Quarterly* study noted, "Although applied to many different contexts, including medicine, pornography, and the workplace, among others (Haslam, 2006), **people commonly dehumanize others of a different race to theirs,** and often strip racial outgroups members of their humanity, thus likening them to non-human entities (Goff et al., 2008; Haslam, 2006; Jahoda, 1999). The **dehumanization of Black people** in particular has a long history, **rooted in centuries of oppression and inequality**" (Anderson, Holland, Heldreth, and Johnson, 2018) [bold added]

11 *Psychology of Women Quarterly* study noted, "**One common stereotypical representation of Black women is that of the Jezebel**—an alluring and seductive African American woman who is highly sexualized and valued purely for her sexuality (Donovan, 2007; Jewell, 1993). **According to Jewell (1993), the Jezebel is a "worldly seductress" who "fulfils the sex objectification requirement of white womanhood"** (p. 46). **She is reduced to her body and treated as little more than a tool that exists for the pleasure of others.** Although hypersexuality and many features of the Jezebel stereotype can also be imposed on White women, the notion of the Jezebel is particularly pronounced for Black women, signifying their inferior status (Jewell, 1993)." [bold added]

12 *Psychology of Women Quarterly* study noted, "The Jezebel stereotype was particularly common during slavery (Donovan, 2007), when African American women's bodies were socially controlled as sexual objects based on racist, classist, and sexist ideologies (hooks, 1981). **However, the stereotype still persists today, exemplified in the way Black women are represented in mainstream media. Recent research suggests that Black women are hypersexualized to a greater degree in the media than are White women.**" (Anderson, Holland, Heldreth, and Johnson, 2018) [bold added]

spectators, over everything, towards God,
forward—*beyond. Wonder if we, unfrozen*
active, are the Eighth Wonders of the World.

Have you forgotten about Waco, about
great grandfathers, about today's black
veterans come home to be slaughtered?

I feel freest when on the run on
a rubber belt—nowhere. Everywhere.

Country of Truth strewn wolf
is everyone's nation, located
between the Nile and the Amazon,

the Cincinnati and the Lethe,
the Colorado and the Yellow.

We are the original infantry
dubbed unpatriotic though red
is Georgia's dirt with our blood.

We are refusing to be played,
the young supernova sings in
her own no stadium, a field

barren just off Exit Left West,
sings at black men and white men
and all souls as she cinches cloak,
We are refusing to be played,

and explodes into rain—blue glitter
—escapes underneath a trap door
as the stage is strewn with roses
she has sacrificed not viewing.

She performs under her own name,
like Beyoncé before her, *Tamika*
then pulls the steel plough to eat.

In lieu of Christ, awaiting the
miracle—arrival, be loved by me.

The single black women collect roses
and smell them in silent empty spaces.
Maybe in the fall, maybe in spring,
our bòuquet will be set free—

steel soul
gardens. Artists of alone

and ~~thriving~~ surviving. The Madonna
is the black woman, charged
with constantly healing,

with twins, alternate reality
and bright future. Conjoined.

Gladys Knight sings beautiful
from a beautiful soul surely
the national anthem and blue
tongued spectators *feel together for a minute*

Where the limoncello

Where the blue icy

Where the civilized

Where the cannibals

Smile. Drink a blue
sugary cold. Sip
a blue sugary cold. Cold

blue ice of East Walnut's
hills rise high and I forget
to die a living death,[13] black hermit.

Fans wonder if an Empress of Soul is master,
foreman, or the slave and half-time a
sparkling rhythmic paradise or cage.

13 *Psychology of Women Quarterly,* study noted, "Finally, research also suggests that **the consequences of sexualization,** including **sexual violence, are far greater for Black women than they are for White women.** For instance, **Black survivors of rape** are not only considered more sexually promiscuous than White women (Donovan, 2007), they are also less likely to have the experience defined as rape, are held more responsible, and others are less likely to believe the incident should be reported to authorities, compared to White survivors of rape (Foley, Evancic, Karnik, King, & Parks, 1995). A recent study found that **individuals feel less willing and less obliged to intervene in a situation involving a Black woman at risk of sexual assault,** compared to a situation in which her race is unspecified (Katz, Merrilees, Hoxmeier, & Motisl, 2017)." (Anderson, Holland, Heldreth, and Johnson, 2018) [bold added]

We are not hiring Colin Kaepernick.

Nike is the goddess of victory, chiseled
before Christ and ancient, two millennia old
in the third millennium. The Winged Nike stands
gown windblown and headless in the Louvre as
we stare not at her breasts but her future motion,

flight. Nike hires Colin as iconography in a black
and white photograph as a symbol of loss to gain.
Increase sales overnight. Livid

white consumers burn Nike swooshes, they
burn Nike swooshes as if Nike is a nation.
As if they know no God except purchase
and opinion, they rage ignorance.

Have they seen The Winged
Victory of Samothrace? Do they know God?

Tamika used to play priest until, in Vatican
City, the smallest country in the world, Catholicism's head,
the pope, re-banned women as leads: priest, bishop, pope.
Now, Tamika sings to fans, *There is nothing and*
everything I can say to save everyone at once—

In Rome, gladiators.
In America, gladiators.
The tour guide in Rome says, *No,*
they weren't slaves.

Poor white Americans are slaves
to racism, says Jamaal in history,
the rich erase the poor's sadness

with blackness as worseness.
Here the apple
Bite

Barbaric.
Barbarism.
Apple. Bite.

The black man's ashen rejection
balmed by black-women-as-unlovely.
Here the apple
Bite

There are snakes in the grass.

This is the age of information.
This is the most ignorant
and enlightened age.
These are the Digital Ages.

The finger of the Winged
Nike was found. Her head
is still missing. The Sphinx
has no nose, strange purpose

yet see how humanity merges
with the animal. How a woman
returns to her warm cave at night
coils around Siberian Huskies,
her head seems fused to coats.

Blood lives in the heart's chambers,
marries the lungs and is a fortress,
it keeps her as it is the keep.

Go Bengals, Go Bengals, Go!
the now and the now
and the now now now now now

The stadium is a ruin
Italian pupils believe
stands far more complete
than the Colosseum.[14]

---

14 *"We the People of the United States,
in Order to form a more perfect Union,
establish Justice, insure domestic Tranquility,*

*provide for the common defence,
promote the general Welfare,
and secure the Blessings of Liberty*

*to ourselves and our Posterity,
do ordain and establish this*

*Constitution for the United
States of America."*—Preamble, U.S. Constitution

COMMON SENSE

A counter Girl at Saks Fifth Avenue,
fifty years old and bronze skin
taut, says, *You better work, girl*

to a wealthy widow girl, aged eighty,
crying over blue lipstick
and five-hundred-dollar cedar perfume.

Where the woods

Where the ocean

MIRROR LAKE

It was cold and cold
crept into each orifice.

Smiling into a frozen oval
fountain, a strange face

fractured into mosaic—
as if each man replacing

men who replaced me
with big cities and diseases

threw the wet flesh he stole
into the blue glittering depths.

Strange face, love
of my life. Leaving

this skeleton for
bare buildings and

thin men thinned
into lost architecture.

I was a spineless disciple
of false gods, judges, jobs.

My life drawn like Mirror
Lake, oval and you can circle

it. Oval and you can circle it
several times as wind chimes

from Cincinnati's seven hills
are chorus to this run

around away inside of
Loss. A deepening lonely cry

of the black wolf in Eden Park
resides within itself. So sing

self into Mirror Lake. The voice
echoes and embraces the cured

spectator of the Northeast's lonely
doing and a melody returns

to being green, rooted here,
becomes skin to bone to soul.

I am a tumbleweed blown back
from the turned backs frozen stiff

of the world up East outside East
Walnut Hills—filled world, leaking.

Those who run straight away for love
return home drawing circular ovals.

Such that Jamaal, studying fear,
discovers the cure for loneliness

at the bottom of Mirror Lake—
above the pennies, watery grace,

God this is a face.
God, this is too much water to waste.
God, good God, I am embraced.

At Mirror Lake, we pace and pace
fixed points along a curved line

spines bowed dragging a steel
plough thrown off for the cold dip

our mouths drip, drinking what lies
between the self and another, God!

We say as if to pray. Predators
slink away from joyful laughing.

Each body of water beside another
body of water watering the world.

Mirror Lake is so exquisitely tiled,
a skull in Columbus mosaics then heals

as if what we did for twenty years past
two thousand was Feel and Think
and swipe by our souls for dimes.

My title for it *"This is fine. I am living
my best life"* at Mirror Lake: a pig flies
glazed in quarters and woman-sized.

THE
LIFE

NO SAINT

In East Walnut Hills, rent or buy Human Hive,
stacked cells aglow. We close our eyes
to others' lives, the red curtains blown out

into black January night. At The Branch
restaurant, the gauze drapes' silhouettes
of kept women icing their black eyes,

I love it here.
I think I'll stay.

Big U the aggressor,
little i the apologizer,

to all my enemies
and all my saints,

all my loves
I could not see

underneath white-
crested waves,

beneath the snowy
veil of endless winter,

I apologize and will not
do it again, those petty sins.

little i
Big I

All the well-intentioned,
sorry for I am no saint, no

queen, no princess,
there is no knight, no
savior, no missionary,

there is no rescue so I
learned how to save myself

and in all my saving
left a wake of suffering,
losing myself to grief.

Count the letters
in this book as bounty.

Please, please
forgive me. *Is there no*
such thing as living alone?

An obese wife in red gracefully leans over
her indifferent husband and says *Do you even eat?*
to a bony single mom minding her own business.

I photosynthesize my insecurity, the mother says
as her only child forms and reforms sisterhood

with blue clay under candlelight making
herself her own best friend five times:
big, small, circular, rectangular, and blob.

WIFE: *Oh, be quiet—really?*
SINGLE: *I cannot be kept*
quiet. I am the keep.

Is there no such thing as dying alone
unless you are the last survivor?

The child asks if Ancestor is a great name.
At The Branch, even the rich cry, doubt.

CRUCIBLE STEEL

East Liverpool, OH

In East Liverpool, granddad breathed
his last clean breath. A black WWII vet,
he breathed in a new war, quarter century
of coke particles atop the oven—got Red
Lung and hair. Country drunk, poet. Coil
so quiet, it rolled tons over the factory floor
into bone, crushed the new guy to death.
Not every black man in our family slaved.
Roosie and Alonzo, enlightened, foremen
got offices away from fire. Out the mill, age 66,
delimbed, men died months into retirement.
The black died before the white—worst jobs.
College stint, Dad pinched his thigh, clear tore
flesh between harrow discs—*the 4th of July,*
a double! Their kin: *I barely know what steel is.*
They were good hard paying jobs for there, then.
City and degree slicked, I steel my life with verse.

MARWIN LAKE

for Ahmaud Arbery, Kevin Burks, & Nia Wilson

In East Liverpool, '81, the black boy dances with
a whitewashed wall and the white girl with red hair.
I just wanted to know what it would be like to
kill a n—. (Now, I am a black woman

over twenty yet white men still might
want to stab me in the neck before green
trees and city buses in Oakland, in Queens.)

At Marwin Lake, post-segregation clapped
hands intertwine—piano keys—over red
punch like blood, Everybody's Blood's This Red,
and a Black boy befriends his future white
murderers who burn their own white

noses with cocaine, their own mouths with meth
and 24-pack Schlitz, blue veins flush with heroin,
minds with racist radio, crack blooming white
in glass pipes. They'll wait six years to beat to death

the black boy after growing up with him,
after pretending his heart was long stopped
and his breath went out and when he begged
for his life did they answer, *I just wanted to*

know what it would be like to kill a—. I got
one! I got one but not the one who beat me.
(Now, I cannot make new friends or keep a man. Is it
the beauty myth, roots? Is the answer: Marwin Lake?

At night, I hear the jazz run among the crops
to the red barn gone black—inside: silhouettes
and *I just wanted to know what it would be*
like to what it would be like to justice, peace.

I am safe nowhere. I run among the white houses
and the Black jogger, ex-football, is hunted down
shot by the White men in the white truck like father
like son in the truck bed like father like sin.

I just wanted to know what it would be like, justice,
to dance all night, loved and trustful.
Unworried that the blackest men looking
just beyond the blackest women would be buried
alive by white communities, imprisoned, as

us black girls bleed out our hearts in Birmingham our
male assailants say, *I thought I saw an alien.* I no-no
notice the news not noticing our suffering, deaths.)

I feel like June at Marwin Lake: the ghosts of 1960s
black women, beaten in row houses by all
men, vacationed as civil rights rolled in like fog
from out the humidity of the burned South—
a specter's cape that saved us and did not save us.

In July, at Marwin Lake, the ghosts of 1940s
segregation cackle and slow dance. They
slow slow dance and strangle each other
until somebody's white God does nothing

until somebody's Bad God says nothing
and there is no headline. It rains.

*

Ahmaud Arbery (1994-2020)

Nia Wilson (1999-2018)

Kevin Burks (1962-1987)

*

John Lee Cowell Convicted of First-Degree Murder of Nia Wilson – Sfist.com | Three Suspects in Ohio Murder to be Extradited – San Bernardino Sun | 2 Suspects Charged With Murder in Ahmaud Arbery Shooting – New York Times | Nia Wilson, Killed at BART Station, is Remembered: 'No Peace Without Justice' – New York Times | Burks' Murderer Denied Parole – The Review Online | Ahmaud Arbery was killed doing what he loved, and a south Georgia community demands justice – CNN | Nia Wilson murder trial: John Lee Cowell ruled sane at time of attack, faces life in prison – San Francisco Chronicle | Father and son arrested and charged with murder in death of Ahmaud Arbery – NBC

*

"Injustice anywhere is a threat to justice everywhere."

–Martin Luther King, Jr.

TRENDS

The jewelry department is filling up
with water. There are wildfires out West.

The mannequins are falling over
wetting their immobile breasts,

white and black and Love You
Pink. Will the mannequins
replace humanity? Is god real, sad?

The jewelry department is filling up
with wolves. There's a riot out back.

The intimates department is burning.
Please, miss, measure

my breasts. One day, I'll buy
a new body—a new life and death.

GASLIGHT DISTRICT

Cincinnati, Ohio

In Clifton, Ludlow Street, the gas lamps glow
in dusk like nettle jellies riding black
and white Atlantic sea. They sting my soul,
these lights. Not modern. Goldenrod, bleak.

Alight, I am alight tonight, afraid
of life and dying pain. Nostalgia calls
my name. Under glass celestial day
the night recedes and—swear—my past falls
in fiery balls so warm to present touch.

The here and now is dim without the lamps
which gild exposed skin in hope
from bygone years reminding folks to clutch
their loves unlike lonely summers at camp.

If bygone time is neither good nor bad,
why does the gas lamp reduce sidewalk to sand?

ACKNOWLEDGMENTS

The author wishes to thank the editors of the following publications:

Aquifer: The Florida Review Online: "Santa Maria Novella"

English Journal: "Name"

Cosmonauts Avenue: "Mirror Lake"

Kenyon Review: "I'm Not Interested"

Pleiades: "Crucible Steel"

POETRY: "Marwin Lake," "Sky"

Poetry Northwest: "Neighbor," "Park"

Sonora Review: "Black Laura," "Pedestal"

Sprung Formal: "Shape"

For generous financial and artistic support, the author thanks the Poetry Foundation, Iowa Writers' Workshop, Kenyon Review, Boston University, and The Ohio State University. Paige Lewis, thank you for selecting this book for the Zone 3 Press First Book Award. Thank you dearly to the editors at Zone 3 Press. For encouragement and support, thank you everyone and thank you immensely to Kathy Fagan Grandinetti, Tracie Morris, Claudia Rankine, Elizabeth Willis, Emily Wilson, and especially Natalie Shapero. Thank you, workshop peers and students. Thank you to C and D. Thank you, endlessly, family.

in memory of Mimi

for us

AFTERWORD

This book was written between December 2015 and December 2020. Thank you for reading.

Love,

Emily Spencer

RESOURCES

National Association for the Advancement of Colored People:
naacp.org | 877-622-2798, at time of publication

National Domestic Violence Hotline: thehotline.org | 800-799-7233,
at time of publication

National Sexual Assault Helpline: rainn.org | 1-800-656-4673, at time of publication

National Suicide Prevention Lifeline: suicidepreventionlifeline.org | 800-273-8255,
at time of publication

Crisis Text Line: Crisistextline.org | Text HOME to 741741, at time of publication

Substance Abuse and Mental Health Services Administration Helpline:
www.samhsa.gov | 1-877-726-4727, at time of publication

Family abuse: What it is and how to identify it. Kids Help Phone:
https://kidshelpphone.ca/get-info/family-abuse-what-it-is-and-how-to-identify-it/

Manipulation: Symptoms to Look For. WebMD. www.webmd.com/mental-health/
signs-manipulation

Your Body Is Not an Apology Workbook: Tools for Living Radical Self-Love.
Sonya Renee Taylor. 2021. 978-1523091164